Contents

Draw the Circle

STUDY GUIDE

Also by Mark Batterson

Draw the Circle
Draw the Circle Prayer Journal
Draw the Circle Children's Curriculum (DVD-ROM)
The Circle Maker
The Circle Maker Curriculum (adult, children's)
The Circle Maker for Kids
The Circle Maker Prayer Journal
The Circle Maker Student Edition
Praying Circles Around the Lives of Your Children
All In
All In Curriculum
All In Student Edition
Going All In

Draw the Circle

Taking the 40-Day Prayer Challenge

STUDY GUIDE | FIVE SESSIONS

Mark Batterson

ZONDERVAN

Draw the Circle Study Guide
© 2018 by Mark Batterson

This title is also available as a Zondervan ebook.

Requests for information should be addressed to:
Zondervan, *3900 Sparks Dr. SE, Grand Rapids, Michigan 49546*

ISBN 978-0-310-09466-1

Published in association with the literary agency of Fedd & Company, Inc.
Post Office Box 341973, Austin, TX 78734.

First Printing December 2017 / Printed in the United States of America

How to Use This Guide

Group Size

The *Draw the Circle* video-based study is designed to be experienced in a group setting such as a Bible study, Sunday school class, or other small-group gathering. If you are participating in the study with a larger group, it is recommended that you break up into smaller groups of five to eight people to ensure everyone has enough time to participate in discussions.

Materials Needed

You and each member of the group should have your own copy of this study guide, which includes the opening questions you will discuss, notes for the video teaching segment, discussion questions, and between-sessions personal studies. You and your group should also have a copy of the *Draw the Circle* book, which provides further insights into the material you will be covering in this study. (See the note at the end of each week's personal study for what chapters to read in the book to prepare for the next week's group meeting.)

Facilitation

Your group will need to appoint a person to serve as leader or facilitator. This person will be responsible for starting the video and keeping track of time during discussions and activities. Group leaders may also read questions aloud and monitor discussions, prompting participants to respond while assuring everyone has the opportunity to participate. If you have been chosen for this role, note there are additional instructions and resources in the back of this guide to help you lead your group members through the study.

Personal Studies

During the week, you can maximize the impact of the course with the personal studies provided for each session. These studies are intended to be devotional in nature, so use them in whatever way works best for your schedule. You may wish to do one section each day for three days of the week, or complete them all in one sitting.

Drawing a Circle

I believe prayer is the difference between the best you can do and the best God can do. It's the difference between letting things happen and making things happen. It's the difference between you fighting for God and God fighting for you. Over the next forty days, we're going to pray like it depends on God and work like it depends on us. And I believe that God is going to show up and show off His power, His grace, His goodness. Welcome to the forty-day prayer challenge.

MARK BATTERSON

First Thoughts

Rodney "Gypsy" Smith was born on the outskirts of London in 1860. At the age of sixteen, he made a decision to follow Christ and taught himself to read and write so he could start preaching the message of Jesus. He would often sing hymns to the people he met, earning him the nickname of the "singing gypsy boy."

In time, Gypsy began serving in various missions organizations in England, including the Salvation Army. He crisscrossed the Atlantic Ocean forty-five times, preaching the gospel to millions of people, and he never preached without someone surrendering their life to the lordship of Jesus Christ. It seemed as if everywhere he went, revival was right on his heels.

At one point, Gypsy issued a challenge to those who likewise wanted to see revival. He said, "Go home. Lock yourself in your room. Kneel down in the middle of the floor, and with a piece of chalk draw a circle around yourself. There, on your knees, pray fervently and brokenly that God would start a revival within that chalk circle."

When was the last time you prayed that way?

When you pray fervently and brokenly, the heavenly Father hears your heart. But I would add "consistently" to the equation. So, at the beginning of this forty-day journey, I want to challenge you to pick a *time* and pick a *place* to pray. If it helps, draw a circle somewhere. Or use a hula hoop. Or map out a prayer route that you walk each day. Or write your prayer requests in a journal and circle them. And as you pray *fervently*, *brokenly*, and *consistently*, I encourage you to pray with the *authority* that is yours as a child of God.

As we will discuss this week, God is not a genie in a bottle, and your wish is not His command. Your prayer must meet a twofold litmus test—the *will* of God and the *glory* of God. But if they do, you will pray with the full authority of the King and His kingdom. It's your positional authority in Christ that gives you a holy confidence as you pray.

In Matthew 18:18, Jesus says, "Whatever you bind on earth will be bound in heaven." The word *bind* has a legal connotation. It means "to place a contract on something." This is precisely what happens when you pray in the will of God. You are exercising our authority as believers to stake claim to the promises of God—and those are the kind of prayers that honor God.

Circling things in prayer is binding them on earth.

What do you need to start circling?

Getting Started

Before watching session 1, as a group read, pray, and meditate (RPM) on Joshua 1:1–11:

> ¹ After the death of Moses the servant of the LORD, the LORD said to Joshua son of Nun, Moses' aide: ² "Moses my servant is dead. Now then, you and all these people, get ready to cross the Jordan River into the land I am about to give to them—to the Israelites. ³ I will give you every place where you set your foot, as I promised Moses. ⁴ Your territory will extend from the desert to Lebanon, and from the great river, the Euphrates—all the Hittite country—to the Mediterranean Sea in the west. ⁵ No one will be able to stand against you all the days of your life. As I was with Moses, so I will be with you; I will never leave you nor forsake you. ⁶ Be strong and courageous, because you will lead these people to inherit the land I swore to their ancestors to give them.

⁷ "Be strong and very courageous. Be careful to obey all the law my servant Moses gave you; do not turn from it to the right or to the left, that you may be successful wherever you go. ⁸ Keep this Book of the Law always on your lips; meditate on it day and night, so that you may be careful to do everything written in it. Then you will be prosperous and successful. ⁹ Have I not commanded you? Be strong and courageous. Do not be afraid; do not be discouraged, for the LORD your God will be with you wherever you go."

¹⁰ So Joshua ordered the officers of the people: ¹¹ "Go through the camp and tell the people, 'Get your provisions ready. Three days from now you will cross the Jordan here to go in and take possession of the land the LORD your God is giving you for your own.'"

Take a few minutes to pray and meditate on this passage; then write down your personal reflections. What was one thing that stood out to you from the Scripture? In what ways does that represent a new insight for you?

Watch the Video

Play the video for session 1. As you watch, use the following outline to record any thoughts or concepts that stand out to you.

God's promise to Joshua—and to us

....

....

....

....

The litmus test for our prayers

....

....

....

....

Our authority through prayer

....

....

....

....

The significance of "forty" in Scripture

....

....

....

....

The goal of the forty-day challenge

....

....

....

....

The importance of finding a time, a place, and a problem

....

....

....

....

Group Discussion

Take a few minutes with your group members to discuss what you just watched and explore these concepts in Scripture.

1. At the beginning of this session, I share about my favorite place to pray: the rooftop of Ebenezers Coffeehouse. Where is your favorite place to pray? Is there a place where you pray with a little more faith because of a miracle God has already done? Explain.

   ....

   ....

   ....

   ....

2. Have you ever done a forty-day challenge before—whether forty days of prayer, forty days of purpose, or even a forty-day fast of some sort? What was your experience like? Are there any lessons you learned that will help you this time around?

   ....

   ....

   ....

   ....

3. If you've never done a forty-day challenge, what are your hopes or concerns?

....

....

....

....

4. Reread **Joshua 1:3**. In the video, I share how when I read this verse, God prompted me to do a 4.7-mile prayer walk around the perimeter of Capitol Hill. Have you ever had a promise "jump off" the pages of Scripture and into your spirit? What is a promise you've circled in prayer during some season of life?

....

....

....

....

5. Read **Matthew 18:18** and **Hebrews 4:16**. What instructions regarding prayer do we receive in these verses? In what ways are we to pray?

....

....

....

....

6. The primary purpose of prayer is not to change our circumstances; the primary purpose of prayer is to change *us*. Have you ever tried to "pray away" something? Is there

an unanswered prayer that, in retrospect, you're glad God *didn't* answer?

....

....

....

....

Personal Reflection

Conclude today's session by reflecting on these questions on your own.

1. If you don't know what you want to get out of this forty-day prayer challenge, you probably won't get much out of it. So take a few minutes to brainstorm the people, problems, or promises you want to circle in prayer. Maybe it's a dream that has gathered dust. Perhaps it's a problem that is beyond your ability to solve. Or maybe it's a promise you need to believe God for once again. Write down a short list—three things—that you want to circle in prayer.

    • ....

    • ....

    • ....

2. On a scale of 1 to 10, how would you rate your current prayer life? Do your prayers tend to be infrequent or reserved for emergency situations? Or are you praying consistently?

1	2	3	4	5	6	7	8	9	10

RARELY PRAY   CONSISTENTLY PRAY

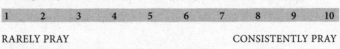

3. Gratitude is thanking God *after* He does something. Faith is thanking God *before* He does it. What is something you need to begin thanking God for—as if He's already done it in your life?

    ....

    ....

    ....

4. Prayer is a *team* sport. Who can you invite into your prayer circle, to partner with you in prayer? Try to identify an Aaron and a Hur—someone who will lift your hands. Then identify a Moses, someone you want to provide prayer support to.
    An Aaron / Hur: ....
    A Moses: ....

Next Steps

In *Draw the Circle*, I discuss the importance of journaling and state that you need to "journal like a journalist." If you don't have a journal, *get* a journal. You will need it to write out your prayers so you have a record of the things you circle during this forty-day challenge.

Remember that prayer isn't about outlining our agenda to God. It's about getting into His presence and His Word and discerning His agenda for you. So, at the beginning of this study, pray about what to pray about. Then take time to listen. Listen to your life. Listen to family and friends. Listen to the still small voice of the Holy Spirit.

Don't rush the listening phase of this process. Don't be afraid of silence. And resolve to do more listening than talking. Put Psalm 46:10 into practice: "Be still, and know that I am God."

As you read through the passages we will discuss in the book of Joshua, ask God if there is a promise He wants you to circle. While you watch the video segments or read *Draw the Circle*, pay close attention to the things that stir your spirit or spark an idea.

It's okay if it takes the first few days or even the first few weeks of the forty-day challenge to identify what it is you want to circle in prayer. Once you identify the person or problem or promise you want to pray for, write that in the circle.

Draw the Circle

DAILY REFLECTIONS

Session 1 Personal Study

In 1952, a Princeton doctoral student asked Albert Einstein a question: "What original dissertation research is left?" I'm intrigued and inspired by Einstein's answer: "Find out about prayer." That is the challenge on the table during this study: *find out about prayer.* My prayer for you is that each day on this journey will yield a new discovery—and that those discoveries will change the way you pray. And when you change the way you pray, everything else changes.

This week, as part of your forty-day challenge, I encourage you to read days 1 to 7 in *Draw the Circle*—one reading each day—and use the questions in this section to reflect on what you've read. Be sure to note these reflections in this guide or your journal, as there will be a time at the beginning of next week's session to share your thoughts with the group.

Day 1: Get Ready

• • • • •

KEY TAKEAWAY: If you pray to God regularly, irregular things will happen on a regular basis.

1. Read **Acts 10:1–8**. What do you learn about Cornelius's prayer habits in this passage? How did this open the door for *irregular* things to happen to him?

    ....

    ....

    ....

    ....

    ....

2. What are some ways that God has invaded the routine of your life as you have sought Him consistently in prayer?

    ....

    ....

    ....

    ....

3. What are some of the dangers of trying to "manufacture your own miracles" instead of waiting for God to act in His timing?

    ....

    ....

    ....

    ....

    ....

Day 2: Established by God

• • • • •

Key Takeaway: God is great not just because nothing is too big for Him; God is also great because nothing is too small.

1. Read **Proverbs 16:9**. How does this verse assure you that God has everything under control? What does it say about our plans versus God's plan?

   ....

   ....

   ....

   ....

2. None of us doubts God's ability to handle the "big things," like keeping the planets in order. But what are some of the "small things" in your life that you tend to doubt God's ability to handle?

   ....

   ....

   ....

   ....

3. What is one small, practical step of obedience that you could take today to show God that you trust Him in the small things?

   ....

   ....

   ....

   ....

Day 3: Amazing Things

• • • • •

KEY TAKEAWAY: If we give more of ourselves to God, God will give more of Himself to us.

1. Read **Matthew 26:36–39**. How did Jesus demonstrate that He was surrendering His will to God's plan in this passage?

   ....

   ....

   ....

   ....

   ....

2. What are some "Garden of Gethsemane" moments in your life where you've had to submit your plans to God?

   ....

   ....

   ....

   ....

   ....

3. What are some things in your life—talent, time, treasure— that you still need to surrender to the lordship of Christ?

   ....

   ....

   ....

   ....

   ....

Day 4: Don't Pray Away

• • • • •

KEY TAKEAWAY: Sometimes God delivers us *from* our problems; sometimes God delivers us *through* our problems.

1. Read **John 9:1–5**. How did Jesus "set the record straight" about why the man in this story had been born blind?

   ....
   ....
   ....
   ....
   ....

2. What is the difference between *praying away* and *praying through*? Which types of these prayers do you tend to pray?

   ....
   ....
   ....
   ....
   ....
   ....

3. What is a situation in your life where you saw God change *you* through it rather than simply make the problem go away?

   ....
   ....
   ....
   ....
   ....
   ....

Day 5: Write It Down

· · · · ·

KEY TAKEAWAY: The shortest pencil is longer than the longest memory.

1. Read **Habakkuk 2:2–3**. What reasons did God give to Habakkuk as to why he should write down the revelations that he was receiving?

   ....

   ....

   ....

   ....

   ....

2. What do you do to document what God has been doing in your life?

   ....

   ....

   ....

   ....

   ....

3. What are some things in your life that—as you look back now—you can see how God carefully determined your steps?

   ....

   ....

   ....

   ....

   ....

   ....

Day 6: Shameless Audacity

• • • • •

KEY TAKEAWAY: The greatest tragedy in life is the prayers that go unanswered simply because they go unasked.

1. Read **Luke 11:5–8**. What was Jesus's point in telling this parable?

   ....

   ....

   ....

   ....

   ....

2. What are some examples of times when you've prayed with "shameless audacity"?

   ....

   ....

   ....

   ....

   ....

   ....

3. What are some areas in which you need to hand over the control to God?

   ....

   ....

   ....

   ....

   ....

   ....

Day 7: Put on Waders
· · · · ·

KEY TAKEAWAY: If you want to see God move, make a move.

1. Read **Matthew 14:25–33**. What does this story tell you about stepping out in faith *first* to witness God move?

   ....
   ....
   ....
   ....
   ....

2. How have you seen God move in your life when you were willing to step out in faith?

   ....
   ....
   ....
   ....
   ....

3. What small step of faith do you feel God is calling you to take today?

   ....
   ....
   ....
   ....
   ....

Dream Big

*What promise are you circling? What miracle
are you believing God for? Whatever it is that
you're circling during this series, you need to
make sure it is bigger than you are. That's how
God gets the glory! He does things that are
beyond our ability, and beyond our resources,
so we can't take credit for it. Two things about
God that I know to be true are that God is
bigger than big and God is closer than close.
And those two realities shape our prayer life.*

MARK BATTERSON

First Thoughts

Show me the size of your dream, and I'll show you the size of your God.

In Isaiah 55:8–9, God likens the difference between our thoughts and His thoughts to the expanse of space. "'For my thoughts are not your thoughts, neither are your ways my ways,' declares the LORD. 'As the heavens are higher than the earth, so are my ways higher than your ways and my thoughts than your thoughts.'"

Translation: your best thought on your best day is at least 15.5 billion light years short of how great and how good God really is! In theological terms, this is called the *transcendence* of God. God is bigger than big! But that's a little intimidating if left by its lonesome. The good news is there is a theological counter-balance to that bigness, and it's called the *immanence* of God. God is also closer than close.

In Psalm 36:5–6, David writes, "God's love is meteoric, his loyalty astronomic, his purpose titanic, his verdicts oceanic. Yet in his largeness, nothing gets lost; not a man, not a mouse, slips through the cracks" (MSG).

God is great not just because nothing is too big. God is also great because nothing is too small.

Our big dreams honor God because they warrant His divine intervention, but don't dismiss the importance of praying about "little things." If those things weren't important to God, He wouldn't know the number of hairs on your head (see Luke 12:7).

Praying is a form of dreaming, and dreaming is a form of

praying. The more you pray, the bigger your dream will become. And the bigger your dream becomes, the more you have to pray! It's big dreams that keep you on your knees in raw dependence on God.

God-sized dreams are just that—beyond your resources and beyond your ability to make them possible. But these kinds of dreams give God the opportunity to show up and show off His power. Nothing will keep you in a posture of prayer like a big dream.

So . . . what is your God-sized dream?

Getting Started

Before watching session 2, as a group read, pray, and meditate (RPM) on Joshua 6:1–5:

> ¹ Now the gates of Jericho were securely barred because of the Israelites. No one went out and no one came in.
>
> ² Then the LORD said to Joshua, "See, I have delivered Jericho into your hands, along with its king and its fighting men. ³ March around the city once with all the armed men. Do this for six days. ⁴ Have seven priests carry trumpets of rams' horns in front of the ark. On the seventh day, march around the city seven times, with the priests blowing the trumpets. ⁵ When you hear them sound a long blast on the trumpets, have the whole army give a loud shout; then the wall of the city will collapse and the army will go up, everyone straight in."

Take a minute to pray and meditate on this passage; then write down your personal reflections. What was one thing that stood out to you from the Scripture?

....

....

....

....

Now take a few moments to review any reflections you recorded from the readings (days 1–7) you completed in Draw the Circle *during the week. What are some of the insights you wrote down that you would like to share with the group?*

....

....

....

....

Watch the Video

Play the video for session 2. As you watch, use the following outline to record any thoughts or concepts that stand out to you.

Our earliest memories leave an imprint on our soul.

....

....

....

....

God is able to do more than we can ask or imagine.

....

....

....

....

Start talking to your problems about God.

....

....

....

....

The difference between gratitude and faith

....

....

....

....

God's will, God's way, God's time

....

....

....

....

God is great because nothing is too small.

....

....

....

....

....

....

Group Discussion

Take a few minutes with your group members to discuss what you just watched and explore these concepts in Scripture.

1. What is your earliest memory as a child? Do you feel like it has had a significant impact on who you are? Explain.

    ....

    ....

    ....

    ....

    ....

    ....

2. Read **Ephesians 3:20–21**. What does Paul say in these verses about how you are to pray? When is a time when God answered your prayer in a greater way than you imagined?

    ....

    ....

    ....

    ....

    ....

    ....

3. What is the bravest prayer that you could pray right now? Why?

....

....

....

....

4. Prayer involves talking to God about your problems. But what does it mean to talk to *your problems* about God? How would that shift your focus in prayer?

....

....

....

....

5. Read **Revelation 12:11**. In the video, note how this verse says we overcome by "the word of our testimony." What is a two-minute testimony you could share with the group about a prayer God has answered or a prayer you are praying right now?

....

....

....

....

6. Read **Luke 12:6–7** and **Psalm 139:4**. What do these verses tell you about God's presence in your day-to-day life? What is something "small" in your life that you need to take to God?

....

....

....

....

Personal Reflection

Conclude today's session by reflecting on these questions on your own.

1. In Luke 18:1–8, Jesus tells the story of a persistent widow. She takes desperate measures in her search for justice, and God honors her "crazy faith." What does persistence in prayer look like in your life? Provide an example or two.

....

....

....

2. Think about how desperate you are for the blessing, the breakthrough, or the miracle. How are you like or unlike the persistent widow? Are you desperate enough to pray through the night? How many times are you willing to circle the promise? How long will you knock on the door of opportunity? Until your knuckles are raw? Until you knock the door down? On a scale of 1–10, rate how desperate you are for God right now.

| 1 | 2 | 3 | 4 | 5 | 6 | 7 | 8 | 9 | 10 |

NOT DESPERATE   VERY DESPERATE

3. The way you steward God's miracles is by believing in Him for even bigger and better miracles. What miracles has God already done in your life? What are the bigger and better miracles you still need to believe Him for?

....

....

....

4. Think about that person in your life who tries your patience—that person who gets on your nerves and requires extra grace. Have you tried circling them in prayer? Will you commit to pray for them this week to see if it changes your heart toward them (and maybe even your circumstances)?

....

....

....

Next Steps

In *Draw the Circle*, I note that there "comes a moment when you must quit speaking to God about the mountain in your life and start speaking to the mountain about your God." That's what I did on July 2, 2016, when God healed my asthma.

What is the bravest prayer you could pray right now?

By definition, God-sized dreams are beyond your ability, beyond your resources, and beyond your logic. If God doesn't do it, it can't be done. And it's those God-sized dreams that honor God, because you can't take credit for them.

What mountain do you need to speak to?

What promise do you need to stand on?

What truth do you need to declare?

In Zechariah 4:7, God tells the prophet, "What are you, mighty mountain? . . . You will become level ground." But then God gives Zechariah an important reminder: "Don't despise the day of small beginnings" (see verse 10). Big dreams usually start with small steps of faith, but those small steps of faith can turn into giant leaps. And if you do little things like they're big things, God will do big things like they're little things!

According to rabbinic tradition, when God told Noah to build the ark, the first thing he did was plant trees! After all, he knew he'd need lots of lumber. That's how things start in God's kingdom. You have to sow the seed. Generally speaking, dreams don't happen at the speed of light. They happen at the speed of a seed planted in the ground that has to take root before it can bear fruit.

What is the first step you can take toward your dream? Note it here.

....

....

....

....

Draw the Circle

DAILY REFLECTIONS

Session 2 Personal Study

This week, as part of your forty-day challenge, I encourage you to read days 8 to 14 in *Draw the Circle*—one reading each day—and use the questions in this section to reflect on what you've read. Be sure to note these reflections in this guide or your journal, as there will be a time at the beginning of next week's session to share your thoughts with the group.

Day 8: One God-Idea

• • • • •

Key Takeaway: One God-idea is worth more than a thousand good ideas.

1. Read **Job 12:7–8**. What are some methods God has used in your experience to illuminate His ideas and bring them to life?

   ....

   ....

   ....

   ....

   ....

2. How would you describe the difference between *good* ideas and *God*-ideas?

   ....

   ....

   ....

   ....

   ....

3. How big do you view God in your life? How would having a bigger view of Him and His power impact the way you pray?

   ....

   ....

   ....

   ....

   ....

Day 9: Dream Factory

• • • • •

KEY TAKEAWAY: Never underestimate the power of a single prayer.

1. Read **2 Corinthians 10:5**. What does it mean to "take captive" every thought and make it obedient to Christ? What does that look like in your life?

   ....
   ....
   ....
   ....

2. What are some ways you are capturing *creative* thoughts and using them for God?

   ....
   ....
   ....
   ....

3. What are some ways you are being obedient to make those God-dreams a reality?

   ....
   ....
   ....
   ....
   ....

Day 10: Crazy Faith

• • • • •

KEY TAKEAWAY: Bold prayers honor God and God honors bold prayers.

1. Read **Luke 5:17–26**. What kind of "crazy faith" did the friends of the paralyzed man reveal in this story? How did Jesus respond to their bold faith?

   ....

   ....

   ....

   ....

   ....

2. What are some "desperate measures" you've taken to get an answer from God?

   ....

   ....

   ....

   ....

   ....

3. When bold prayers become the norm in your life, so do the miraculous breakthroughs that follow. What are some bold prayers you need to pray today?

   ....

   ....

   ....

   ....

   ....

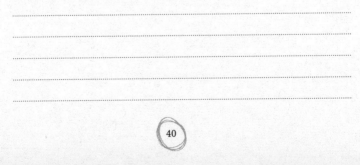

Day 11: First-Class Noticer

• • • • •

KEY TAKEAWAY: We don't see the world as it is; we see the world as we are.

1. Read **1 Corinthians 13:12.** What does it mean to be "watchful" in prayer?

....

....

....

....

....

2. As you look back, how have you seen God give you "spiritual eyes" to notice the things that matter most to Him?

....

....

....

....

....

3. What are some new things God has caused you to notice as you've started this forty-day challenge? How have you seen these things in a new light?

....

....

....

....

....

....

Day 12: Sow a Seed

· · · · ·

KEY TAKEAWAY: If we do the little things like they are big things, then God will do the big things like they are little things.

1. Read **Luke 17:5–6**. A mustard seed was the smallest known garden seed in the culture of the day, while a mulberry tree could grow more than fifty feet in height. What is Jesus saying about the power of even a little bit of faith?

   ....

   ....

   ....

   ....

   ....

2. What are some examples in your own life of how God answered in a big way when you prayed with even just a little bit of faith?

   ....

   ....

   ....

   ....

3. How do you view prayer as "planting a seed" that might bear fruit during your lifetime?

   ....

   ....

   ....

   ....

Day 13: One Day

• • • • •

KEY TAKEAWAY: God can accomplish more in one day than you can accomplish in a lifetime.

1. Read **2 Peter 3:8–9**. What do these verses say about God's timing?

    ....

    ....

    ....

    ....

    ....

2. When was a time you tried to "manufacture" a miracle instead of waiting on God and persevering in prayer? What was the result?

    ....

    ....

    ....

    ....

    ....

3. How have you seen God stretch your faith so you can dream bigger dreams?

    ....

    ....

    ....

    ....

    ....

    ....

Day 14: Speak to the Mountain
• • • • •

Key Takeaway: Quit talking to God about your problem and start talking to your problem about God.

1. Read **Matthew 17:20**. What are "mountains" in your life that you need to have removed? What does this passage say about God's ability to handle those problems?

....

....

....

....

2. Think about your "pharaohs"—those people who get in the way of what God wants to do in your life (see Exodus 7:13). How do you tend to deal with them?

....

....

....

....

3. What are some ways you can turn your anger against "impossible people" into prayer for them? How easy or difficult is this for you to do?

....

....

....

....

Pray Hard

By definition, praying hard is hard. In God's kingdom, prayer is the heavy lift. But prayer is the difference between "good ideas" and "God-ideas." It's the difference between closed doors and open doors. It's the difference between impossible and possible. But you can't just pray like it depends on God. You also have to work like it depends on you. What I mean by that is this: you can't just talk the talk—you also have to walk the walk.

MARK BATTERSON

First Thoughts

We have a tendency to confuse our job and God's job. We want to do amazing things for God, but that isn't our job. That's God's job! He is the One who does amazing things for us. Our job is to *consecrate* ourselves. And if we do our job, God is going to do His job.

A key piece of that consecration process is prayer. And that means not just "praying for" but "praying through." Prayer is the difference between us fighting for God and God fighting for us. God wants to fight our battles for us, but we have to pray through till the breakthrough. As Jesus said, "Ask and it will be given to you; seek and you will find; knock and the door will be opened to you. For everyone who asks receives; the one who seeks finds; and to the one who knocks, the door will be opened" (Matthew 7:7–8).

The story of God delivering on His promise to Abraham and Sarah in the book of Genesis is a quick and easy read. It only takes a few minutes to get from God's promise to make them "into a great nation" (12:2) to the fulfillment when Sarah "bore a son to Abraham in his old age" (21:2). But Abraham and Sarah weren't *reading it*, they were *living it*. Those twenty-five years had to feel like an eternity! How did they endure?

In Romans 4:18, Paul provides the answer: "Against all hope, Abraham in hope believed." Is there a situation in your life where you need to not just hope, but *hope against hope*—to pitch your tent in the land of hope? Is there some situation that requires more than just "praying for," but actually "praying through"?

It's time to hit your knees, and then hang on to the promise in Philippians 1:6: "He who began a good work in you will carry it to completion."

Getting Started

Before watching session 3, as a group read, pray, and meditate (RPM) on Joshua 3:1–8:

¹ Early in the morning Joshua and all the Israelites set out from Shittim and went to the Jordan, where they camped before crossing over. ² After three days the officers went throughout the camp, ³ giving orders to the people: "When you see the ark of the covenant of the LORD your God, and the Levitical priests carrying it, you are to move out from your positions and follow it. ⁴ Then you will know which way to go, since you have never been this way before. But keep a distance of about two thousand cubits between you and the ark; do not go near it."

⁵ Joshua told the people, "Consecrate yourselves, for tomorrow the LORD will do amazing things among you."

⁶ Joshua said to the priests, "Take up the ark of the covenant and pass on ahead of the people." So they took it up and went ahead of them.

⁷ And the LORD said to Joshua, "Today I will begin to exalt you in the eyes of all Israel, so they may know that I am with you as I was with Moses. ⁸ Tell the priests who carry the ark of the covenant: 'When you reach the edge of the Jordan's waters, go and stand in the river.'"

Take a minute to pray and meditate on this passage; then write down your personal reflections. What was one thing that stood out to you from the Scripture?

....

....

....

....

Now take a few moments to review any reflections you recorded from the readings (days 8–14) you completed in Draw the Circle during the week. What are some of the insights you wrote down that you would like to share with the group?

....

....

....

....

Watch the Video

Play the video for session 3. As you watch, use the following outline to record any thoughts or concepts that stand out to you.

We're only two feet from revival.

....

....

....

....

A definition of faith

....

....

....

....

What it means to be consecrated to God

....

....

....

....

Faith is taking the first step.

....

....

....

....

Pray like it depends on God, but work like it depends on you.

....

....

....

....

Prayer must lead to action.

....

....

....

....

Group Discussion

Take a few minutes with your group members to discuss what you just watched and explore these concepts in Scripture.

1. Have you ever "contended" for something in prayer? If so, what happened?

    ....

    ....

    ....

    ....

2. In the video, I tell the story of a young Billy Graham, who, while visiting the childhood home of John Wesley, prayed, "O Lord, do it again!" What are some revivals you need God to "do again" in your life? What do you need Him to do in your family's lives?

    ....

    ....

    ....

    ....

3. Read **Matthew 5:23–24**. Jesus tells us to leave our gift at the altar if someone has something against us and be reconciled.

Has God ever interrupted you while you were praying? Have you ever experienced this kind of prompting during prayer?

....

....

....

....

4. In the video, I note that one of the great mistakes we make is asking God to do for us what He wants us to do for Him. Have you ever made that mistake? Explain.

....

....

....

....

5. Read **Mark 16:20**. The last words of Mark's Gospel are "signs following" (KJV) or "signs that accompanied it" (NIV). Have you ever had God give you a sign confirming something you believe He asked you to do? What made you think it was from God?

....

....

....

....

6. How did receiving this sign from God affect your faith? How did it impact your life?

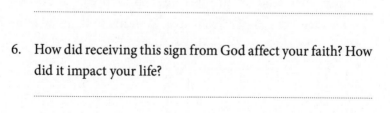

....

....

....

....

Personal Reflection

Conclude today's session by reflecting on these questions on your own.

1. There is a distinction between "praying for" and "praying through." On a scale of 1–10, rate how you would characterize your prayer life right now.

| 1 | 2 | 3 | 4 | 5 | 6 | 7 | 8 | 9 | 10 |

PRAY FOR   PRAY THROUGH

2. There are some things you don't need to pray about—you just need to go do them. Is there something you need to stop praying about and start doing something about?

3. One of my prayer mantras is, "Lord, surprise me!" What would this prayer look like in your life? What are some ways that God could "surprise" you? (Try praying this prayer this week. Ask God to surprise you, and keep your eyes open for supernatural synchronicities. Be ready to share with the group how God answers that prayer!)

4. If you are waiting to do something God has asked you to do because you feel you are not ready, there's a good chance you'll be waiting the rest of your life. In other words, you'll never be ready! Is there something God has called you to do, but you've delayed obedience because you're not sure if you're ready? What is it?

....

....

....

....

Next Steps

In Joshua 3:8, God gives the people a curious command: "Go and stand in the river."

We want God to part the river before we step into it so we don't have to get our feet wet, but God wants us to take a step of faith. And that's where most of us get stuck spiritually. We're waiting for God to make a move, while God is waiting for us to make a move!

Faith is taking the first step before God reveals the second step. We can't just pray like it depends on God—we also have to work like it depends on us. After we kneel and pray, we've got to get up and take a step of faith. We have to step into the Jordan River!

The Bible wasn't just meant to be read. It was meant to be prayed through, meditated on, and acted upon! We have to employ the action-oriented approach to Scripture advocated by Peter Marshall, who said, "I wonder what would happen if we all agreed to read one of the Gospels, until we came to a place that told us to do something, then went out to do it, and only after we had done it . . . began reading again?"

Why not give that a try this week?

Ebenezers Coffeehouse has served more than a million customers and given more than one million dollars in net profits to kingdom causes. But it started out as an eighty-five-dollar step of faith at an auction. I placed a bid on a book outlining zoning rules and regulations. I knew I could buy a copy for less money *after* I got a contract on the property, but I felt I needed to demonstrate my faith and purchase the book *before* we got the contract.

If we hadn't been able to get the property, it would have been a complete waste of money. But I believed that God was going to give it to us, so I acted on it by making that eighty-five-dollar bid. I got the book—and a few months later, we got the contract on the property.

What step of faith do you need to take?

What river do you need to step into?

Draw the Circle

DAILY REFLECTIONS

Session 3 Personal Study

This week, as part of your forty-day challenge, I encourage you to read days 15 to 21 in *Draw the Circle*—one reading each day—and use the questions in this section to reflect on what you've read. Be sure to note these reflections in this guide or your journal, as there will be a time at the beginning of next week's session to share your thoughts with the group.

Day 15: Contend for Me

· · · · ·

Key Takeaway: Prayer is the difference between you fighting for God and God fighting for you.

1. Read **Psalm 35:1, 23**. What do these verses say about the way God contends for you when you are fighting for His cause?

2. What does it look like in your life to let God fight your battles for you? How easy or difficult is it for you to give up your problems to God?

3. What is the problem with engaging in the combat of criticism? Why does this tend to be a no-win situation for everyone involved?

Day 16: Lord, Surprise Me

• • • • •

KEY TAKEAWAY: God always has a holy surprise up His sovereign sleeve.

1. Read **Acts 12:5–16**. How did God surprise the believers who had been praying?

    ....

    ....

    ....

    ....

2. In what ways would asking God to "surprise you" be a dangerous prayer? What would it require on your part to honestly say this prayer to God?

    ....

    ....

    ....

    ....

3. How has prayer added an element of surprise to your life? What other surprises are you asking God to provide for you?

    ....

    ....

    ....

    ....

    ....

Day 17: Do Not Delay

• • • • •

KEY TAKEAWAY: God is never early. God is never late. God is always right on time.

1. Read **Numbers 23:19**. What does this verse say about God and His promises?

....

....

....

....

....

2. If you stand *on* God's Word, God will stand *by* His Word. What are some promises from God that you can pray with holy confidence?

....

....

....

....

....

3. Why do you think God sometimes delays in answering our prayers? What value have you seen in praying ALAT ("as long it takes") kinds of prayers?

....

....

....

....

....

Day 18: Keep Circling

• • • • •

KEY TAKEAWAY: If you don't get out of the boat, you'll never walk on water.

1. Read **2 Chronicles 20:15–17**. How did the Lord encourage His people in the face of an overwhelming army that was marching against them?

    ....

    ....

    ....

    ....

    ....

2. When is a time God has encouraged you to persevere when you have wanted to give up? How has God proven the battle was *His* to fight?

    ....

    ....

    ....

    ....

    ....

3. What is potentially at stake if you *don't* keep circling in prayer for something God has put on your heart?

    ....

    ....

    ....

    ....

    ....

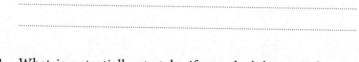

Day 19: Memorial Offerings

• • • • •

KEY TAKEAWAY: Our prayers don't die when we do. God answers them forever.

1. Read **Psalm 141:2.** How are our prayers like an offering to God?

   ....

   ....

   ....

   ....

   ....

2. How do you respond to the thought that your prayers live on after you die? How does this affect the way you think about prayer?

   ....

   ....

   ....

   ....

   ....

3. How are you making intercessory prayer part of the spiritual DNA of your family?

   ....

   ....

   ....

   ....

   ....

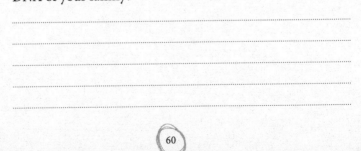

Day 20: Go. Set. Ready.

• • • • •

KEY TAKEAWAY: If you are looking for excuses, you will always find one.

1. Read **Hebrews 11:8–12**. How did God honor Abraham's faith when he answered God's call "even though he did not know where he was going"?

   ....
   ....
   ....
   ....
   ....

2. How do you balance making wise plans and taking a risk to step out in faith? Recall a time God prompted you to act even when you didn't feel fully prepared.

   ....
   ....
   ....
   ....
   ....

3. What is the first step or next step you need to take in the journey God has called you to travel? What are you doing to move in that direction?

   ....
   ....
   ....
   ....

Day 21: Set Your Foot

· · · · ·

KEY TAKEAWAY: God is not a genie in a bottle, and your wish is not His command. His command better be your wish.

1. Read **James 1:5–6**. How are you instructed to pray in these verses?

   ....

   ....

   ....

   ....

2. Drawing prayer circles starts with discerning what God wants. How have you been seeking His discernment as you've circled items during this forty-day challenge?

   ....

   ....

   ....

   ....

3. What are some other areas God has prompted you to "lay claim to" as you've undertaken this challenge?

   ....

   ....

   ....

   ....

Think Long

We can't dream big without thinking long. We often want God to do things at the speed of light, but in God's kingdom, things happen at the speed of a seed planted in the ground that has to take root before it can bear fruit. This is about trusting His timing—and with the Lord, "A day is like a thousand years, and a thousand years are like a day" (2 Peter 3:8). We need more patience and more persistence . . . and that's a byproduct of time and experience.

MARK BATTERSON

First Thoughts

In 1785, a French mathematician named Charles Joseph Mathon de la Cour wrote a parody mocking Benjamin Franklin's optimism. Franklin was the founder of the *Poor Richard's Almanac,* the most widely read periodical in eighteenth-century America. De la Cour fictionalized about "Fortunate Richard" leaving a small sum of money in his will, to be used only after it had collected interest for five hundred years.

De la Cour was trying to poke fun at Franklin's optimism, but instead of taking offense, the seventy-nine-year-old Franklin wrote De la Cour a letter and thanked him for his excellent idea. Before his death on April 17, 1790, Benjamin Franklin bequeathed a thousand pounds to his hometown of Boston and a thousand pounds to his adopted city of Philadelphia. It wasn't a huge sum of money, but it was given with one stipulation. It was to be placed in a fund that earned interest and supported the public good for two hundred years. Then, and only then, could the funds be released.

For two hundred years, Franklin's endowment earned interest. At the end of that time, both funds were valued at approximately twenty million dollars.

It was Benjamin Franklin who said, "A penny saved is a penny earned." He understood the power of compound interest. Franklin said, "Money makes money. And the money that money makes, makes money." Compound interest is the difference between you working for your money and your money working for you. And it doesn't just apply to finances!

There is a compound interest to our prayers! When a prayer is answered, it accrues interest by starting a domino chain reaction. And our prayers don't die when we do! Prayer has no expiration date. You never know when or where or how God will answer, but He always answers.

Prayer is playing the long game. Why? Because our prayers are eternal.

Getting Started

Before watching session 4, as a group read, pray, and meditate (RPM) on Joshua 14:6–12:

> ⁶ Now the people of Judah approached Joshua at Gilgal, and Caleb son of Jephunneh the Kenizzite said to him, "You know what the Lord said to Moses the man of God at Kadesh Barnea about you and me. ⁷ I was forty years old when Moses the servant of the Lord sent me from Kadesh Barnea to explore the land. And I brought him back a report according to my convictions, ⁸ but my fellow Israelites who went up with me made the hearts of the people melt in fear. I, however, followed the Lord my God wholeheartedly. ⁹ So on that day Moses swore to me, 'The land on which your feet have walked will be your inheritance and that of your children forever, because you have followed the Lord my God wholeheartedly.'
>
> ¹⁰ "Now then, just as the Lord promised, he has kept me alive for forty-five years since the time he said this to Moses, while Israel moved about in the wilderness. So here I am today, eighty-five years old! ¹¹ I am still as strong today as the day Moses sent me out; I'm just as vigorous to go out to battle now as I was then. ¹² Now give me this hill country that the Lord promised me that day. You yourself heard then that the Anakites were there and their cities were large and fortified, but, the Lord helping me, I will drive them out just as he said."

*Take a minute to pray and meditate on this
passage; then write down your personal
reflections. What was one thing that stood out
to you from the Scripture?*

....

....

....

....

*Now take a few moments to review any reflections
you recorded from the daily readings you
completed in* Draw the Circle *during the week.
What are some of the insights you wrote down that
you would like to share with the group?*

....

....

....

....

Watch the Video

Play the video for session 4. As you watch, use the following outline to record any thoughts or concepts that stand out to you.

Dream big, pray hard . . . and think long.

....

....

....

....

Praying ALAT—"as long as it takes"

....

....

....

....

Caleb was fighting a battle for future generations—as we are.

....

....

....

....

We don't plant seeds of faith for ourselves.

....

....

....

....

God remembers His promise to David . . . six kings later.

....

....

....

....

The greatest tragedy in life

....

....

....

....

Group Discussion

Take a few minutes with your group members to discuss what you just watched and explore these concepts in Scripture.

1. Read **1 Kings 18:41–46**. Have you ever thought God said *no* to a prayer, but it turned out to be a *not yet*? What does this story tell you about praying for an answer ALAT—for as long as it takes?

    ....

    ....

    ....

    ....

2. In the video, I share the story of an African American pastor who prayed with so much authority and intimacy with God that, by comparison, it seemed as if I had never prayed. This man's example also inspired me to get to know God that way. Have you ever known someone like this? Someone who is closer to God than you are? Someone who inspires you to pray with more authority and more confidence? Explain.

    ....

    ....

    ....

    ....

3. Read **Luke 11:1–4**. Clearly, the disciples had prayed before and knew how it was done. So why do you think they were making this request? What were they looking for Jesus to provide in asking Him to "teach" them to pray?

4. In the video, I share how my grandfather had a profound impact on me when I heard him pray for his family. Is there someone in your life who has left such a legacy of prayer? How have that person's prayers impacted you?

5. What God does for you is never just for you! It's also for the next generation. Have you ever reaped where someone else has sown? Have you ever been blessed in a way that you know you don't deserve? Share it with the group.

6. Your prayers will live on long after your time on this earth is over. What are you doing to leave a lasting legacy of prayer for others?

Personal Reflection

Conclude today's session by reflecting on these questions on your own.

1. What are some prayers you've prayed for which you received a *no*, *yes*, and *not yet* answer from God? Write these below.

   No: ....

   Yes: ....

   Not yet: ....

2. Think for a moment about the way you typically make requests to God. Do you tend to pray ASAP—as soon as possible—prayers? Or do you pray ALAT—as long as it takes—prayers? Rate yourself on your tendencies on a scale of 1–10.

1	2	3	4	5	6	7	8	9	10

   ASAP   ALAT

3. Walter Wink said, "History belongs to the intercessors." Who are the intercessors who have shaped your life? How have they shaped your life?

   ....

   ....

   ....

4. Have you ever experienced "the sleeper effect"? Are there blessings that you believe trace back to someone else's prayers? Explain.

   ....

   ....

   ....

Next Steps

According to rabbinic tradition, when the twelve spies were doing reconnaissance in the Promised Land, Caleb split off from the group and visited the place where Israel's matriarchs and patriarchs were buried—Abraham and Sarah, Isaac and Rebekah, Jacob and Leah. It was called the Cave of Machpelah, and it was located in the hills of Hebron.

I can picture a forty-year-old Caleb falling on their graves, and swearing on their graves, that he'd be back to claim the land they were buried in. That's where he is forty years later!

Now let me fast-forward.

Caleb wasn't just claiming Hebron for himself or his family. More than five hundred years later, David would be crowned king in Hebron. "David also took the men who were with him, each with his family, and they settled in Hebron and its towns. Then the men of Judah came to Hebron, and there they anointed David king over the tribe of Judah" (2 Samuel 2:3–4).

Hebron was David's first capital. So Caleb was staking claim to Hebron for King David. What God does for us, He's doing for the next generation! He doesn't just answer prayers once. He answers them over and over and over again.

The question is this: *What are we doing that will make a difference a hundred years from now?*

Draw the Circle

DAILY REFLECTIONS

Session 4 Personal Study

This week, as part of your forty-day challenge, I encourage you to read days 22 to 28 in *Draw the Circle*—one reading each day—and use the questions in this section to reflect on what you've read. Be sure to note these reflections in this guide or your journal, as there will be a time at the beginning of next week's session to share your thoughts with the group.

Day 22: Prayer Fleece

• • • • •

Key Takeaway: When God gives a vision, He always makes provision.

1. Read **Judges 6:33–40**. How did Gideon ask God to confirm His promises? How did the Lord respond to these requests?

   ....
   ....
   ....
   ....
   ....

2. When is it appropriate to offer a "prayer fleece" to God and ask for His confirmation? What are some cautions in doing this?

   ....
   ....
   ....
   ....
   ....

3. What are some signs you've received in the past when you've asked God for confirmation to your prayers? How did this encourage you to continue?

   ....
   ....
   ....
   ....
   ....

Day 23: Not Now

• • • • •

KEY TAKEAWAY: Sometimes God's *no* simply means *not yet.*

1. Read **Acts 1:4–5**. Why did Jesus instruct His disciples to wait instead of immediately striking out to share the gospel? What might have happened if they didn't wait?

   ....

   ....

   ....

   ....

   ....

2. When have you received an answer to prayer that you thought was a *no* but was actually a *not yet*? What did you learn through the experience?

   ....

   ....

   ....

   ....

   ....

3. How does it help to know that waiting doesn't delay God's plans and purposes but will always expedite them in your life?

   ....

   ....

   ....

   ....

   ....

   ....

Day 24: Find Your Voice

· · · · ·

KEY TAKEAWAY: If you want to find your voice, you need to hear the voice of God.

1. Read **2 Timothy 3:14–17**. How does Paul instruct Timothy on how to know the voice of God and continue to walk in His ways?

    ....

    ....

    ....

    ....

    ....

2. What are some ways you have heard God speak to you through His Word?

    ....

    ....

    ....

    ....

    ....

3. How do you reduce the "noise" in your life so you can hear God's voice?

    ....

    ....

    ....

    ....

    ....

    ....

Day 25: A Prophetic Voice
· · · · ·

KEY TAKEAWAY: Prayer is the way we recognize potential in others.

1. Read **1 Corinthians 14:3–4**. What does Paul say is the value of "prophesying" among believers in Christ?

   ....

   ....

   ....

   ....

   ....

   ....

2. How has prayer helped you recognize the potential in others?

   ....

   ....

   ....

   ....

   ....

3. How do you see yourself as a "prophet" in the lives of your family and friends?

   ....

   ....

   ....

   ....

   ....

   ....

Day 26: Game with Minutes

• • • • •

Key Takeaway: Change of pace + change of place = change of perspective.

1. Read **1 Thessalonians 5:16–18**. What do you think it looks like to "rejoice always," "pray continually," and "give thanks in all circumstances"?

    ....

    ....

    ....

    ....

2. What are some ways you pray for people as you go through your day? How has this affected your relationships with them?

    ....

    ....

    ....

    ....

3. If you want God to do something new in your life, you cannot keep doing the same old thing. What are some ways you will mix up how and when you pray this week?

    ....

    ....

    ....

    ....

Day 27: Double Circle

• • • • •

KEY TAKEAWAY: If you want to break the sin habit, you've got to establish a prayer habit.

1. In **Matthew 17:18–21**, the disciples asked Jesus why they had been unable to cast out a demon from a child. Jesus replied, "This kind does not go out except by prayer and fasting" (verse 21 NKJV). What does this tell you about the level of spiritual warfare that was taking place in this situation?

....

....

....

....

....

2. What do you think of when you hear the word *fast*? What is the value of fasting from something when it comes to the effectiveness of your prayers?

....

....

....

....

3. What are some things you need to "double circle" with prayer and fasting?

....

....

....

....

Day 28: Quit Praying
• • • • •

KEY TAKEAWAY: Don't just pray about it; do something about it.

1. Read **James 2:14–17**. What does James say about faith without actions when it comes to serving others?

....

....

....

....

....

2. In what ways can praying become a form of spiritual procrastination? What evidence of this have you seen in your own life?

....

....

....

....

....

3. When is a time in your life when God has instructed you to quit praying about something and get to work on doing it?

....

....

....

....

....

The Ripple Effect

*Over the past few weeks, we've been dreaming
big, praying hard, and thinking long. We've
been circling people and problems and
promises. But the goal wasn't just circling for
forty days—it was also to still be praying on
day forty-one. There is no expiration date
on prayer! Every prayer you pray has a chain
reaction, and those chain reactions set off a
thousand other chain reactions. Every prayer
you pray ripples all the way into eternity!*

MARK BATTERSON

First Thoughts

In 1936, Harvard professor Robert K. Merton published a paper titled "The Unanticipated Consequences of Purposive Social Action." Merton was one of the founding fathers of modern-day sociology, and over the course of his career he published some fifty papers in his field. However, perhaps his most famous—and most enduring—contribution was his modernization and popularization of the "law of unintended consequences."

Simply put, this law states that the outcome of our purposive actions have unintended consequences beyond our ability to control and beyond our ability to predict. Those unforeseen consequences fall into two basic categories.

On the negative side, there are unexpected drawbacks, like the side effect of a medicine that cures a condition while causing complications.

On the positive side of the ledger, there are added bonuses called unexpected benefits. That's when things turn out better than we could have imagined, like when the side effect of a medicine not only treats a current condition but helps prevent another more serious condition. And that's where the omniscience of God comes into play!

It's hard for us to imagine the ramifications of our actions and our decisions—and that goes for prayer too. The good news? When you approach everything with "prayer and petition," as Paul exhorts us to do in Philippians 4:6, there are bound to be unexpected benefits! Why? Because God is able to do immeasurably more than all we can ask or imagine.

Prayer can stop a vicious cycle that spirals out of control and has detrimental results. It can also start a virtuous cycle by turning the momentum and reinforcing favorable results.

Getting Started

Before watching session 5, as a group read, pray, and meditate (RPM) on Joshua 4:1–7:

> ¹ When the whole nation had finished crossing the Jordan, the LORD said to Joshua, ² "Choose twelve men from among the people, one from each tribe, ³ and tell them to take up twelve stones from the middle of the Jordan, from right where the priests are standing, and carry them over with you and put them down at the place where you stay tonight."
>
> ⁴ So Joshua called together the twelve men he had appointed from the Israelites, one from each tribe, ⁵ and said to them, "Go over before the ark of the LORD your God into the middle of the Jordan. Each of you is to take up a stone on his shoulder, according to the number of the tribes of the Israelites, ⁶ to serve as a sign among you. In the future, when your children ask you, 'What do these stones mean?' ⁷ tell them that the flow of the Jordan was cut off before the ark of the covenant of the LORD. When it crossed the Jordan, the waters of the Jordan were cut off. These stones are to be a memorial to the people of Israel forever."

Take a minute to pray and meditate on this passage; then write down your personal reflections. What was one thing that stood out to you from the Scripture?

....

....

....

....

Now take a few moments to review any reflections you recorded from the daily readings you completed in Draw the Circle during the week. What are some of the insights you wrote down that you would like to share with the group?

....

....

....

Watch the Video

Play the video for session 5. As you watch, use the following outline to record any thoughts or concepts that stand out to you.

Our prayers don't dissipate but compound interest over time.

....

....

....

Prayer isn't linear but exponential.

....

....

....

The difference between letting things happen and making things happen

....

....

....

The longest pencil is longer than the longest memory.

....

....

....

Don't underestimate the power of a single prayer.

....

....

....

When you pray to God regularly, irregular things happen on a regular basis.

....

....

....

....

....

Group Discussion

Take a few minutes with your group members to discuss what you just watched and explore these concepts in Scripture.

1. Read **Matthew 20:29–34**. In verse 32, Jesus asks the blind men, "What do you want me to do for you?" How would you answer that question right now? What are you asking God to do in your life?

....

....

....

....

....

2. Have you ever physically circled something in prayer? If so, share the story.

....

....

....

....

....

3. Like the Israelites in Joshua 4, have you ever built an altar to God? Or kept a memento from some experience to remind you of something God did? Explain.

....

....

....

....

....

4. Read **Deuteronomy 6:20–23**. Why does God instruct His people to remember they were "slaves of Pharaoh in Egypt"? How does this relate to keeping His commands?

....

....

....

....

....

5. Why is it important to treat the "little things" in prayer like they were "big things"? How would treating all of your prayers with this importance impact the way you pray?

....

....

....

....

....

6. In the video, I state, "I think someday we'll thank God as much for the prayers He doesn't answer as the ones He does." How do you respond to this statement? Looking back,

are there any prayers you're now glad God didn't answer the way you wanted?

....

....

....

....

....

Personal Reflection

Conclude today's session by reflecting on these questions on your own.

1. In the video, I note that prayer is the difference between "letting things happen" and "making things happen." On a scale of 1–10, where do you fall on that spectrum?

1	2	3	4	5	6	7	8	9	10

LETTING THINGS HAPPEN   MAKING THINGS HAPPEN

2. The key to spiritual growth is developing healthy and holy routines—what are known as "spiritual disciplines." What are some healthy prayer routines you have developed?

....

....

....

....

....

3. Spiritual disciplines are good for spiritual growth—but once the routine becomes routine, you have to change the routine.

Is there a spiritual routine you need to change? If so, what is it, and how will you change it?

_____

_____

_____

_____

4. An inheritance is leaving something *for* someone. A legacy is leaving something *in* someone. What do you want your legacy on earth to be?

_____

_____

_____

_____

Next Steps

We tend to remember what we should forget and forget what we should remember. That's why God had the Israelites build an altar at Gilgal with stones from the Jordan River. God wanted to make sure the next generation would not forget what He did there.

Is there an altar you need to build?

One reason why it's important to keep track of your prayers by writing them down is so you don't fail to give God credit. But tracking your prayers also provides a written record for those who come behind you. George Müller may have set the standard with his thirty thousand prayers that he recorded as being answered. Why not follow suit?

At the end of this forty-day prayer challenge, I hope you realize this is just the beginning! Again, the goal wasn't to just pray for forty days and then stop here at the end of this study. The goal wasn't to give God a forty-day deadline to get your prayer answered. No, the goal is to keep on praying in the coming days, weeks, months, and years ahead. It's to keep on praying prayers that might only be answered long after you are gone.

Those prayers are your legacy!

Is it possible that God wants to bless someone 117 years from now through your prayers? Is it possible He wants to do for you what He did for David? But it's 100 percent guaranteed that God won't answer the prayers you don't pray. As I've said, the greatest tragedy in life are the prayers that go unanswered because they go unasked.

The Israelites had to circle Jericho thirteen times over the course of seven days before the walls fell down. Naaman had to dip in the Jordan river seven times before he was healed. Nehemiah had to arm his workers and persevere in the face of enemy attacks to rebuild the walls of Jerusalem. Even Jesus had to pray for the blind man of Bethsaida twice.

Don't give up too quickly or too easily.

Keep circling!

Draw the Circle

DAILY REFLECTIONS

Session 5 Personal Study

This week, as part of your forty-day challenge, I encourage you to read days 29 to 35 in *Draw the Circle*—one reading each day—and use the questions in this section to reflect on what you've read. Note these reflections in this guide or your journal, and consider sharing your insights with a fellow group member in the near future.

Day 29: A New Prayer

· · · · ·

KEY TAKEAWAY: If you want God to do something new, you cannot keep doing the same old thing.

1. Read **Psalm 96:1** and **Matthew 6:7**. What do these verses say about the way God wants to hear from us in prayer?

....

....

....

....

....

2. How do you worship God with not only your memory but also your imagination? Why does God call you to sing a "new song" when it comes to expressing your love for Him?

....

....

....

....

....

3. How do you inject your own personality when it comes to prayer?

....

....

....

....

Day 30: Abide in Me

• • • • •

KEY TAKEAWAY: Reading without meditating is like eating without digesting.

1. Read **John 15:5–8**. What promises does Jesus give when you choose to abide in Him? How does abiding in Christ bring God glory?

    ....

    ....

    ....

    ....

2. What are some ways that you abide in God's Word? How has memorizing and meditating on Scripture helped you in understanding His will?

    ....

    ....

    ....

    ....

3. You can't do something for God if you're not with God on a regular basis. What habits have you instilled to make sure you are abiding with God throughout your day?

    ....

    ....

    ....

    ....

Day 31: Spell It Out

· · · · ·

Key Takeaway: Most of us don't get what we want because we don't know what we want.

1. Read **Mark 10:46–52.** What did Bartimaeus ask of Jesus? Why do you think Jesus responded in the way He did?

    ....

    ....

    ....

    ....

    ....

2. Why do you think God wants you to be specific with your prayers?

    ....

    ....

    ....

    ....

    ....

3. How would you respond if Jesus asked today, "What do you want Me to do for you"? Briefly spell out below some of the dreams that God has placed on your heart.

    ....

    ....

    ....

    ....

    ....

    ....

Day 32: Get a Testimony

• • • • •

KEY TAKEAWAY: Most of us are educated way beyond the level of our obedience.

1. Read **John 4:28–30, 39–42.** How did the Samaritan woman's testimony influence those in her town? How did they respond?

    ....

    ....

    ....

    ....

    ....

2. What is the power of a first-person testimony to what God has done? Why are these more powerful than secondhand or more generic stories of God's grace?

    ....

    ....

    ....

    ....

    ....

3. When we share a testimony, we are "loaning our faith" to others. What are some answered prayers that you need to share with others to loan your faith?

    ....

    ....

    ....

    ....

    ....

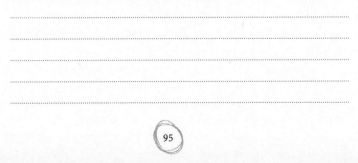

Day 33: Prayer Covering

· · · · ·

KEY TAKEAWAY: If you intercede for others, make sure others are interceding for you.

1. Read **Matthew 18:19–20**. What is the power of several believers in Christ coming together and agreeing in prayer? What promises are we given?

   ....

   ....

   ....

   ....

2. Who are some people you are interceding for in prayer? What specifically are you asking God to do or provide in their lives?

   ....

   ....

   ....

   ....

3. Who are some people you know who are interceding for you? What specifically do you need to request them to pray to happen in your life?

   ....

   ....

   ....

   ....

Day 34: Raise Up a Remnant

• • • • •

KEY TAKEAWAY: When the prayer meeting becomes the most important meeting, revival is around the corner.

1. Read **2 Kings 19:30–31**. How does this represent a promise for all generations?

   ....

   ....

   ....

   ....

   ....

2. What kind of revival do you want to see take place in your world? What are you willing to commit to do in prayer to make that happen?

   ....

   ....

   ....

   ....

   ....

3. When have you unexpectedly seen a move of God in response to prayer? How has this encouraged you to persevere?

   ....

   ....

   ....

   ....

   ....

Day 35: The Longest Level

• • • • •

Key Takeaway: If we do the ordinary, God will add an extra to it.

1. Read **Luke 21:1–4**. Why is it important to God that we offer whatever we have to Him, even if it seems small by the world's standards?

   ....

   ....

   ....

   ....

   ....

2. A key to prayer is to "stay humble and stay hungry." How have these two attributes served in your prayer life? How do you deal with issues of pride that can rise up?

   ....

   ....

   ....

   ....

   ....

3. How have you seen God use humble beginnings in your life for something great in His purposes and plans?

   ....

   ....

   ....

   ....

   ....

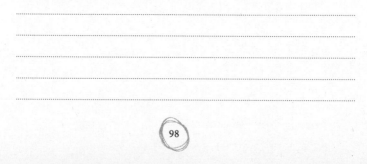

Keep Going!

Complete your forty-day prayer challenge by reading days 36 to 40 in *Draw the Circle*, again using the questions provided to help you reflect what you read. Then keep going! Remember, the goal of the prayer challenge is to establish a prayer habit so you're still praying on day 41, day 61, day 101 . . . and every day for the rest of your life.

Day 36: Senior Partner

• • • • •

KEY TAKEAWAY: What we keep we ultimately lose; what we give away we ultimately get back.

1. Read **Matthew 6:20**. What does it mean to "store up" treasures in heaven?

   ....
   ....
   ....
   ....
   ....

2. The same God who worked in the lives of the men and women in the Bible is the same God at work in your life today. How does this help you to trust in Him completely?

   ....
   ....
   ....
   ....
   ....

3. What are some things in your life that you still need to surrender completely to God? What is keeping you from turning those things over to Him?

   ....
   ....
   ....
   ....
   ....

Day 37: Prayer Contracts

• • • • •

Key Takeaway: Agreeing with someone in prayer is like getting your prayer notarized.

1. Read **Matthew 16:18–19**. What do Jesus's words to Peter tell us about the power that we have been given in prayer?

    ....

    ....

    ....

    ....

    ....

2. To bind in prayer means to place a contract on something in the spiritual realm. What specifically have you been binding in prayer during this forty-day challenge?

    ....

    ....

    ....

    ....

    ....

3. What does it mean to "negotiate" with God through intercession? How has negotiating in this manner increased your faith in God?

    ....

    ....

    ....

    ....

    ....

Day 38: Climb the Watchtower

• • • • •

KEY TAKEAWAY: Going back to places of spiritual significance can help us find our way forward again.

1. Read **Habakkuk 2:1**. In the ancient world, watchmen would stand at their guard posts on top of the city walls and scan the horizon for enemies. How has a habit of daily prayer increased your "sight" into the spiritual realm?

    ....

    ....

    ....

    ....

    ....

2. Answered prayer gives us the courage to pray bigger and bolder prayers. How have you seen your answered prayers embolden you to dream even bigger for God?

    ....

    ....

    ....

    ....

3. What are some places of spiritual significance that you revisit? How do these locations remind you of all that God has done for you in the past?

    ....

    ....

    ....

    ....

Day 39: Holy Ground
• • • • •

KEY TAKEAWAY: The purpose of prayer is not to give orders to God; the purpose is to get orders from God.

1. Read **Exodus 3:1–5**. Where was Moses when God called him? What was the significance of God's instruction to Moses to remove his sandals?

    ....

    ....

    ....

    ....

    ....

2. Moses had led a routine existence for forty years when God called him. How have you seen God break in and interrupt your daily routines since you started this challenge?

    ....

    ....

    ....

    ....

    ....

3. How do you view your time with God as "holy ground"? What boundaries have you put in place to continually protect this divine appointment with God?

    ....

    ....

    ....

    ....

Day 40: Prayer Alphabet

• • • • •

KEY TAKEAWAY: Prayer is the difference between the best we can do and the best God can do.

1. Read **Romans 8:26–27**. How does the Holy Spirit help us with our prayers? How have you seen God reward the efforts you've made in prayer?

    ....

    ....

    ....

    ....

2. As you near the end of this forty-day challenge, how has God changed your perceptions of prayer? How have you seen God move in your life?

    ....

    ....

    ....

    ....

3. What ways have you found during these past forty days to turn wherever you are—the classroom, board room, locker room, conference room—into a prayer room?

    ....

    ....

    ....

    ....

Leader's Guide

Thank you for agreeing to lead a small group through this study! What you have chosen to do is valuable and will make a great difference in the lives of others.

Draw the Circle is a five-session study built around video content and small-group interaction. As the group leader, just think of yourself as the host of a dinner party. Your job is to take care of your guests by managing all the behind-the-scenes details so that when everyone arrives, they can just enjoy time together.

As the group leader, your role is not to answer all the questions or reteach the content—the video, book, and study guide will do most of that work. Your job is to guide the experience and create an environment where people can process, question, and reflect—not receive more instruction.

Make sure everyone in the group gets a copy of the study guide. This will keep everyone on the same page and help the process run more smoothly. If some group members are unable to purchase the guide, arrange it so that people can share the resource with other group members. Giving everyone access to all the materials will position this study to be as rewarding an experience as possible. Everyone should feel free to write in their study guides and bring them to the group every week.

Setting Up the Group

As the group leader, you'll want to create an environment that encourages sharing and learning. A church sanctuary or formal classroom may not be as ideal as a living room, because those locations can feel formal and less intimate. No matter what setting you choose, provide enough comfortable seating for everyone, and, if possible, arrange the seats in a semicircle so everyone can see the video easily. This will make transition between the video and group conversation more efficient and natural.

Also, try to get to the meeting site early so you can greet participants as they arrive. Simple refreshments create a welcoming atmosphere and can be a wonderful addition to a small-group meeting. Try to take food and pet allergies into account to make your guests as comfortable as possible. You may also want to consider offering childcare to couples with children who want to attend.

Finally, be sure your media technology is working properly. Managing these details up front will make the rest of your group experience flow smoothly and provide a welcoming space in which to engage the content of *Draw the Circle*.

Starting Your Group Time

Once everyone has arrived, it's time to begin the group. Here are some simple tips to make your group time healthy, enjoyable, and effective.

First, begin the meeting with a short prayer, and remind the group members to put their phones on silent. This is a way to make sure you can all be present with one another and with God. Then, give each person one or two minutes to respond to the questions in the "Getting Started" section. You won't need much time in session 1, but beginning in session 2, people will likely need more time to share their insights from their daily reflections. Usually, you won't answer the discussion questions yourself, but you should go first with the "Getting Started" questions, answering briefly and with a reasonable amount of transparency.

At the end of session 1, invite the group members to complete the daily reflections for that week. Explain that you will be providing some time before the video teaching next week for anyone to share insights. Let them know sharing is optional, and it's no problem if they can't get to some of the reflection activities some weeks. It will still be beneficial for them to hear from the other participants and learn about what they discovered.

During the "Getting Started" section, help the members who completed the daily reflections to debrief their experiences. Debriefing something like this is a bit different from responding to questions based on the video, because the content comes from the participants' real lives. The basic experiences that you may want the group to reflect on are:

- What did I learn about myself?
- What did I learn about God?
- How did this change the way I view prayer?

There are specific questions written to help process each activity, but feel free to expand on this time or adapt the questions based on the dynamics of your group.

Leading the Discussion Time

Now that the group is engaged, it's time to watch the video and respond with some directed small-group discussion. Encourage all the group members to participate in the discussion. As the discussion progresses, you may want to follow up with comments such as, "Tell me more about that," or, "Why did you answer that way?" This will allow the group participants to deepen their reflections and invite meaningful sharing in a non-threatening way.

Note that you have been given multiple questions to use in each session, and you do not have to use them all or even follow them in order. Feel free to pick and choose questions based on either the needs of your group or how the conversation is flowing. Also, don't be afraid of silence. Offering a question and allowing up to thirty seconds of silence is okay. It allows people space to think about how they want to respond and also gives them time to do so.

As group leader, you are the boundary keeper for your group. Do not let anyone (yourself included) dominate the group time. Keep an eye out for group members who might be tempted to "attack" folks they disagree with or try to "fix" those having struggles. These kinds of behaviors can derail a group's momentum, so they need to be steered in a different direction. Model active listening and encourage everyone in your group to do the same. This will make your group time a safe space and create a positive community.

The group discussion leads to a closing time of personal reflection. Invite the group members to take a few minutes to answer some or all of the questions in this section. This will help them cement the big ideas in their minds as you end the session. Close your time together with prayer as a group.

Thank you again for taking the time to lead your group. You are making a difference in the lives of others and having an impact on the kingdom of God.

Draw the Circle

The 40 Day Prayer Challenge

Mark Batterson

Do you pray as often and as boldly as you want to? There is a way to experience a deeper, more passionate, persistent, and intimate prayer life.

Drawing from forty days of true stories, Mark Batterson applies the principles of his *New York Times* bestselling book *The Circle Maker* to teach us a new way to pray. As thousands of readers quickly became many tens of thousands, true stories of miraculous and inspiring answers to prayer began to pour in, and as those stories were shared, others were bolstered in their faith to pray with even more boldness.

In *Draw the Circle*, through forty true, faith-building stories of God's answers to prayer, daily Scriptures and prayer prompts, Batterson inspires you to pray and keep praying like never before. Begin a lifetime of watching God work. Believe in the God who can do all things. Experience the power of bold prayer and even bolder faith in *Draw the Circle*.

The Circle Maker

Praying Circles Around Your Biggest Dreams and Greatest Fears

Mark Batterson

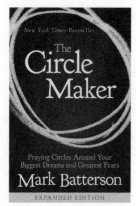

According to Pastor Mark Batterson in this expanded edition of *The Circle Maker*, "Drawing prayer circles around our dreams isn't just a mechanism whereby we accomplish great things for God. It's a mechanism whereby God accomplishes great things in us."

Do you ever sense that there's far more to prayer than what you're experiencing? It's time you learned from the legend of Honi the Circle Maker—a man bold enough to draw a circle in the sand and not budge from inside it until God answered his impossible prayer for his people.

What impossibly big dream is God calling you to draw a prayer circle around?

Sharing inspiring stories from his own experiences as a circle maker, Mark Batterson will help you uncover your heart's deepest desires and God-given dreams and unleash them through the kind of audacious prayer that God delights to answer.

This expanded edition of *The Circle Maker* also includes Batterson's newest insights on how God answers prayer along with stories that add convincing proof to the reality that God is able to do exceedingly far greater than all we could ask or imagine.

ALSO AVAILABLE: Adult and Children's Curriculum

Available in stores and online!